LOVE
BITTER
AND
Sweet

*

David Lord Porter

Carroll & Graf Publishers, Inc.
New York

To LHP
all love's loveliness

Copyright © 1997 by David Lord Porter
All rights reserved

First Carroll & Graf edition 1997

Carroll & Graf Publishers, Inc.
19 West 21st Street
New York, NY 10010

LIBRARY OF CONGRESS CATALOGING-IN-PUBLICATION DATA
Porter, David Lord, 1944–
    Love bitter and sweet / David Lord Porter.
        p. cm.
    ISBN 0-7867-0470-5
    I. Title
    PN6110.L6P65   1997
    811'.54—dc21   97-17489
                                                        CIP

Manufactured in the United States of America

CONTENTS

INTRODUCTION

The following advertisement appeared in the *Boston Transcript* of February 9, 1847:

"English Valentines, per Hibernia.

A.S. Jordan, No. 2 Milk Street, respectfully informs his friends that he has just received by the above steamer the greatest assortment of Valentines to be found in Cupid's regions, among which may be found the following kinds: Sentimental, Lovesick, Funny, Burlesque, Curious, Characteristic, Humorous, Beautiful, Heart-Struck, Witty, Arabesque, Courting, Serio-Comical, Bewitching, Poetical, Heart-Rending, Love-Encouraging, Trifling, Cariacature, Heart-Piercing, Serio-Tragical, Laughable, Silly, Spiteful, Original, Enlivening, Heart-Aching, Despairing, Raving-Mad, Heart- Killing, High-Flown, Lampooning, Romantic, Look-Out, Proposal, Espousal, Matrimonial, Hen-Pecking, Suicidal and many other varities. Wholesale buyers would do well to call before purchasing elsewhere, as the selection has been made by one of the first London houses engaged in that particular business."

Popular at the same period, indeed for fifty years on either side of 1847, was the Valentine Writer. This was a collection of varied sentiments sold to aid one who, rendered inarticulate by love or innate dullness, could then copy out the appropriate sentiment in a valentine of his/her own choosing, or making. The squalid spawn of these antique effusions now squat on shelves of "personalized" greeting cards that address all aspects of the Intimate Relationship. There, one may effortlessly combine the banal and the fatuous to convey precisely one's absolute lack of wit, taste and desireability.

The present slender volume is intended as an antidote to this sucrose overdose. Herein you will discover cariacatures that capture the likeness of Love in more than a few of her infinite guises. If you find, alas, that a preponderance of these sentiments favor the star-crossed more than the starry-eyed, the salacious more than the salubrious, don't blame me. Blame Cupid. It is he that has an instinct for both the jocular and the jugular.

GOD'S RECIPE FOR MAN

Take one angel.

Un-wing it.

Thing it.

GOD'S RECIPE FOR WOMAN

Take one man.

Un-thing it.

Wing it.

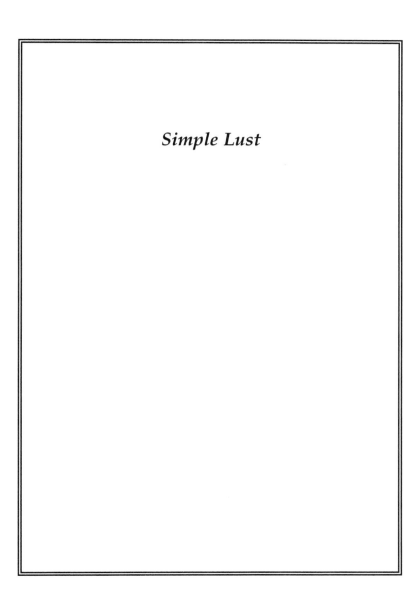

Simple Lust

Cupid's darts strike others' hearts;
Why must he hit me in the private parts?

*

Einstein said Time
*   and Space are curved;*
your curves sublime
*   he n'er observed.*
Had he upon your
*   hourglass stared*
he'd have been sure:
*   "shE = mc ^{2}!"*

*

Had we but world enough and time
This coyness, Lady, were no crime.
But since it's late, I prithee, tell:
My place, or yours, or a motel?

*

Love is a vice. For it we sell
Our souls the hottest seats in hell.
Lust is a virtue. To be precise,
The way most taken to paradise.

You ask me, "What's your angle?"
I answer, "If you please,
Lean back a little farther
And we'll make isoceles."

*

Let me be your Y
Let your X be mine
Let's coordinate
In a valentine:
My vertical line
Intersects your X
Horizontal position
Becomes your sex.

*

You want me now? Don't hesitate:
No circumstances mitigate.

*

You burn for me, but idealize:
You only undress me with your eyes.
Were I to grant you what you covet,
Do you think you could rise above it?

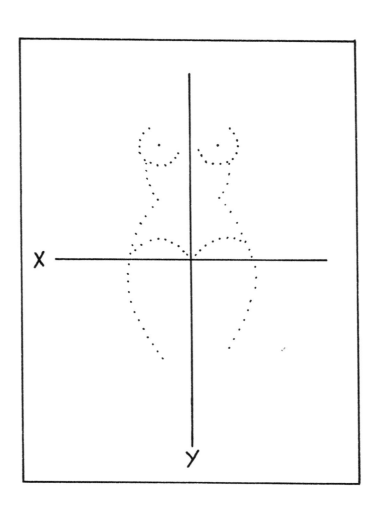

*If you'd encourage
Thoughts unholy,
Turn and walk away.
But, slowly.*

*

*Our predicament is absurd:
Two nouns yearning for a verb.*

*

*You're not bad,
I've seen better;
Worth a card
Not worth a letter.
Worth a whistle:
Fairly curvy;
No epistle.
But, noteworthy.*

*

*Your Cupid's Arrow, to euphemize,
Took me right between the, well... eyes.*

I cannot endure one more detour
From the allure of your curvature.

*

You too, déjà vue?
Once more, en corps?

*

I find your point so...
Penetrating;
Would you much mind...
Elaborating?

*

"Phal - lic" is a sound
That's subtly trillable:
The accent's hard on
The second syllable.

*

Misses' kisses propitious as these
Elicit illicit felicities

Mistress, do not give me an inch,
For I might then take a mile;
Don't even let me kiss your hand
Lest my lips prove more versatile.

*

You striptease, Darling, in my mind,
There you ever bump and grind:
A strutting, spotlit girl unmatched,
All mine with no G-strings attached.

*

Come Valentine, let me read your hand,
Four fingers, palm and thumb;
Give it me under the table and I'll
Show you the shape of things to come.

*

Fox, minks and lynx,
All fur's forbidden,
Unless you caress
The fur that's hidden.

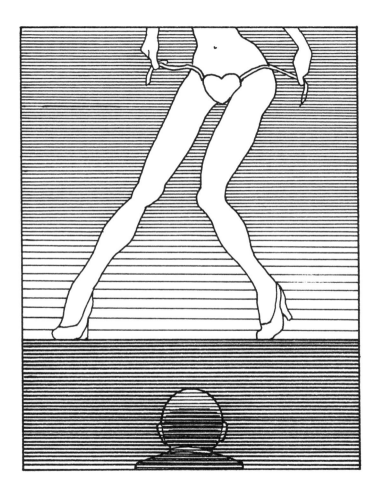

A snowman I
You of snow too
Let us find
Some nice igloo
Where in darkness
Each way turning
I'll show you why my
Coals are burning
Thawing in our
Icy garret
I will melt you
With my carrot.

*

I am just a lad in a lamp,
A genial heart lub-dubbing;
I will take a shine to you,
All it takes is a little rubbing.

*

Museum walls are all bespread
With mistresses, unclothed, abed;
An art lover, I've been pining
To see you in the nude, reclining.

Remember, Dearest, when we two
watched two double-features through,
Neccoing in the furthest reaches,
close as Chicklets made by Beeches:
me bewildered, lovesick, daffy,
you white and soft as Turkish Taffy.
Me daring at last to share your lips'
sweet salt tang of potato chips -
then slight snapping, unwrapping sounds,
you offering to share your Mounds;
me reaching for the Raisinettes
while you watched out for usherettes.
I remember your Jordan Almond eyes,
the hem of your skirt riding up your thighs;
you demonstrated your sweet tooth
by taking hold of my Baby Ruth,
while I delved for life's hidden facts,
the Secret Toy in your Crackerjacks.

Though we've parted, the passion lingers
like the special sweetness of Butterfingers;
those nights were pure dolce far niente,
but what we did was Good n' Plenty.

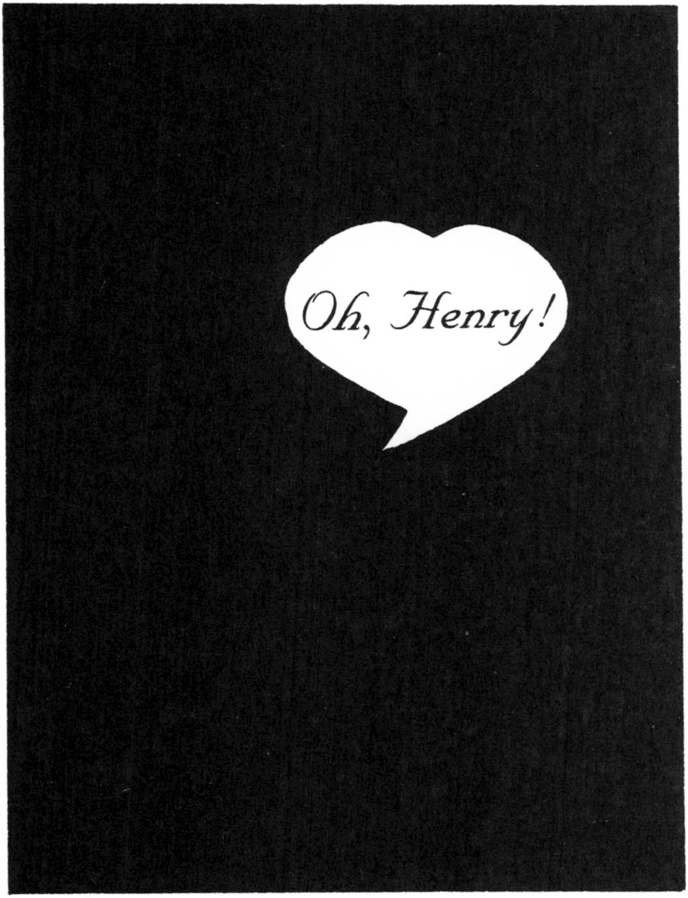
Oh, Henry!

I hate to intrude on your sweet repose,
But I seem to have misplaced all my clothes;
Embarrassed, I couldn't think what to do
But to try to cover myself with... you.

*

At our voltage
    There's no scoffin'
I turn you on
    You turn me often.

*

Archimedes once said
    He'd move the land
If he had a stick and
    A place to stand.
I'll prove Archimedes'
    Worthy scion;
Just agree to be a
    Place to lie on.

*

The Devil makes work for idle hands,
But Oh! what he does for idle glands.

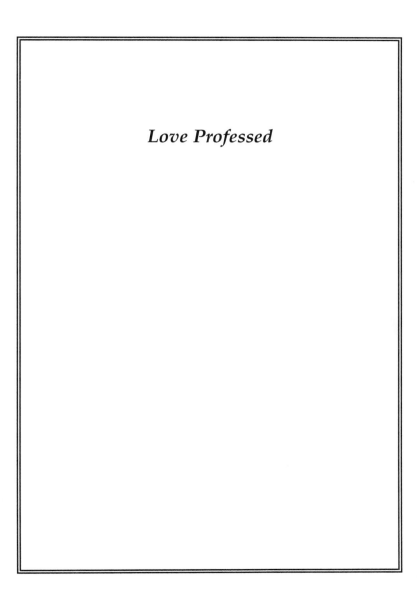

Love Professed

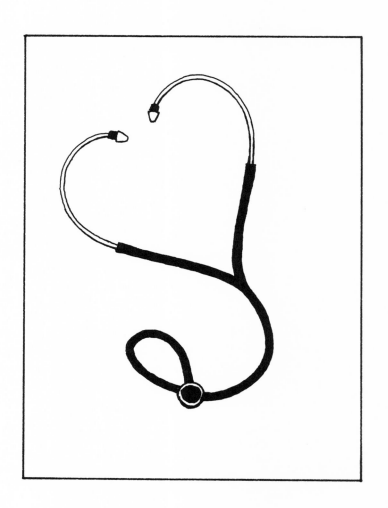

Love-dub! Love-dub!
My heart's hope
Won't have to use
A stethescope.

*

If loving you is thought a crime
I'd be glad to do hard time;
Dearest, if you'd be my bride
I'd go over the wall to get inside;
Darling, if you'd be my wife
I'd be happy serving life;
Shackle me to your ball and chain,
I'd never try to escape again.

*

I know sweet surrender's the proper form,
But I'd rather have you take me by storm.

*

The bow arched back,
The bow-string twanged,
The shaft thus loosed
Then boomeranged.

The first time that I saw you, god!
Cupid let loose a fusillade.

*

You have buried the shaft deeply in me;
I guess that's why I feel so... feathery...

*

Our names in a heart?
Sure, I'm willing:
If I've the best part
And the top billing.

*

You pull with such fierce force on me
(I'm sure it's at least 40 g!)
Jupiter's gravity's between us,
When to me you're merely Venus.

*

The lover vows what he'll if she'll;
I kneel. I will as well, if we'll.

When Cupid made me your valentine
He made me look like a porcupine.

*

Your door's ajar. The sign on mine
doesn't seem like a valentine;
Look closer and perhaps you'll see
I long to share my privacy.
Pay close attention to the verb.
Perhaps it reads **Please Do Disturb**?
Let me give you a little hint:
My love for you has got no "n't".

*

Once I was remote, serene,
secure from love's sick folly;
Since I met you I've been changed
into a hot tamale.

*

Shall I tell you how you make me feel?
Just like a piglet with his first squeal.

Exactitude, Dear, shows what's true,
Precisely, in all cases:
I can quantify my love for you
Down to sixteen decimal places.

*

Reverential
My true love for you
Exponential
The power of 2

*

Because our love has two unknowns
    It must be solved quadratically;
It's so arcane that to be plain
    Must be stated mathematically.
But simple numbers can't express
    My feelings exponential:
I need N's and P's and parentheses
    And a calculus differential.

*

They say 1^2 is still but 1,
They say 1 plus 1 is 2;
But how can 1 be merely 1
If one of those 1's is you?

God and the Devil
I could reunite
My soul's on fire
In heaven tonight

*

Thought I'd take a sip of your love-potion,
Not have to swallow the whole damned ocean!

*

The very page on which I write
Is smoking, yearning to ignite;
I only have to hear your name
To have the room go up in flames.

*

You shake me
Quake me
Make me
Pale
You're at least
9.5
On my Richter
Scale

My Dearest, whenever you murmur "yes"...
It should sound somewhat less like a guess.

*

Don't nibble at me, if you please;
Devour me, if you've got the nerve.
If you drink me, drink me to the lees!
Don't treat me like some damned hors d'ouvre.

*

Love comes but when
It's least looked for:
You draw the blinds
I'll lock the door.

*

Come live with me and be my love
Dearest darling heaven-sent:
Do the laundry, wash the dishes
And we can split the rent.

Just as the Fork said to the Spoon,
Come be my valentine:
I'll tingle your curves till we sing in tune
And you can pluck my tines.

*

My love for you
if it erupts
will be like Krakatoa,
it will burn half
the ocean up
and make some more Samoa.
If you deny me
I'll subside and
vanish like Atlantis;
I'll grow cold
like lavas do in
such sad circumstances.

*

Cupid's blown me right away
To make me this ecstatic
He couldn't have used a bow at all
But a Browning Automatic.

SWF, *hot to trot,*
seeks SWM *w/yacht.*

*

SWM, *for petit déjeuner*
seeks SBF *for café-au-lait.*

*

SWF, *sink or* SWM

*

Some gulp fine wine
But what a waste
And what a bitter
Aftertaste

So let us go
Slowly, my sweet:
Don't chug-a-lug
Chateau Lafitte

I've tied the knot,
I ain't lyin';
But won't you be
My Val un-tyin'?

*

How do I love thee? Let me count the ways:
I'll need Random Access Memory of about 1000 K's.

*

As tunnel to train
Is Woman to Man;
Thus the refrain,
"I think I can!"
"I think I can!"

*

I've been waylaid in Malaysia:
How can I make so light of my plight?
I'm amazed that I feel no malaise:
How can something sarong feel so right?

The Plague of Love

Forget the Ides of March, be wary
Instead of the Ides of February!

∗

I went down the shaft of the deepest mine
To pick and shovel this valentine:
Your heart burns with a lovely light,
But it's black and hard as anthracite.

∗

The arrow true, the bow well-crafted,
The aim sure, the heart, shafted.

∗

Some sing the blues
About their fellow
If I sang hues
Yours would be yellow

∗

Love is not Time's fool, they say,
Until tomorrow or yesterday.

I could find your heart
I could have hope
If I had an electron
Microscope

*

Wading through your tears and guile
I failed to note the crocodile.

*

"Come hither," says
Your Cheshire smile,
Your body fades
Away, the while

*

Let no valentines sing of passion, unsigned!
Who would choose to be wooed by a stranger?
I'd share an igloo with a Tonto I knew
Sooner than wed the Lone f- ing Ranger.

*

Your body my vessel, I am shipwrecked:
I found you went down with all hands on deck.

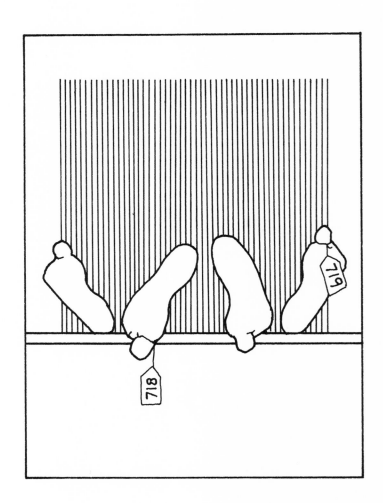

Our love had a prejudicial start:
You were born with an artificial heart.

*

Once I thought you pure as a vestal virgin;
Now I see that you're the vestigial version.

*

When I fell in love with you
I fell into a chasm;
When in turn you fell in love
It was with your orgasm.
Love it seems endureth not,
It's rather episodic;
And even lust, I'm sad to say,
Turns out to be spasmodic.

*

Last night we got carried away;
This morning, pronounced D.O.A.

When you consider the birds
and the bees,
It was a mistake to come down
from the trees.

*

You've got the sway
I've got the swivel
I've got the drool
You've got the drivel

*

That day of white and brightness
Led to this night dark and dank:
We were not walking down the aisle,
We were walking out the plank.

*

You keep my picture
Right next to your bed.
Like a witch-doctor
Keeps a shrunken head.

You entranced me
By necromancy
Now I'm over-fond
Of your magic wand

*

Banjo   bateau   bon mots   Bordeaux
do-si-do   vertigo   bungalow
tally-ho   comme-il-faut
quid-pro-quo
uh-oh
embryo
touch-and-go so and so

*

Your kisses are piddley
Your winks are tiddly
You know a lot
Of diddley-squat

*

Amo	*Tuo*	*I think*
Amas	*Twas*	*I smell*
Amat	*Twat*	*Arat*

"Mighty oaks from acorns grow!"
You swore with bragadoccio:
Your sacred vows were insincere,
Your solid oak, a mere veneer.

*

Men have one string, like a poor puppet:
They must look down your dress, or up it.

*

Your utilitarian philosophy
Made me think your greater good would be me;
Now I see I could not have been dumber:
You're the greatest good for the greatest number.

*

"Now how could I take you to bed," she snapped;
"It's not got a ramp for the handicapped."

*

Our horse was ever before the cart,
Crossed Finish before crossing Start.

Cupid's arrows came so thick and fast in
That I was martyred like Saint Sebastian.

*

Cupid's bow is ever bent
To set some heart aflame:
It isn't that he ever shoots,
It's that he never aims.

*

Cupid hit me with your dart,
I thought it was pneumonia;
Now he's sent another shaft
Demanding alimonia.

*

Your kiss is chaste
You are too young
You don't even know
The French for "tongue"
For me it's just
The same old song
I guess I've been
Around too langue.

Grammar makes my heart a liar:
You're the indirect object of my desire.

*

You find me somewhat cool, aloof?
Can't help myself. I am fool-proof.

*

At the altar we did not linger.
I gave the ring. You gave the finger.

*

In our most intimate relations
You imitate intoxication
I sublimate emasculation
We thus discharge our obligations

*

Love professed with such loquacity
Speaks volumes of a lack of veracity.

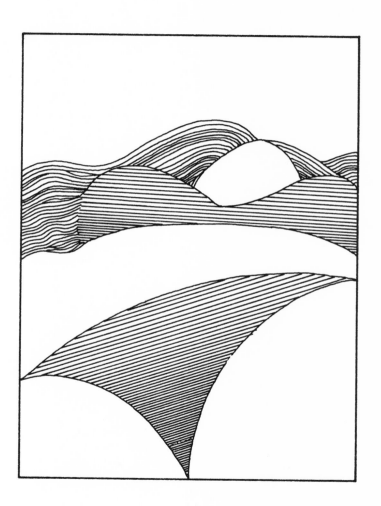

When I undress you with my eyes,
Each hill, each dale, each hummock,
I see your landscape's oversize:
Your thighs are bigger than my stomach.

*

Cordially invited?
R.S.V.P.
But unrequited?
B.Y.O.B.

*

Your qualities have symmetry,
I wonder how you got 'em,
How at the same time you can be
Hard-hearted and rock-bottom.

*

Mirabile Dictu! Darling mine!
You've made tap water out of wine!
A fire so hot none could bank it
You've snuffed out with your wet blanket!

Once, content in your embrace,
I was serene and placid;
Now when I look on your face
I think, "sulfuric acid!"

✳

Ophelia sang of valentines
But found none to adore her;
She took instead to a watery bed,
They're dragging the river for her.

Hamlet's heart he'd given away,
But given it to his mother;
She'd given ring to the late King,
And after that, his brother.

Rosencranz loved Guildenstern,
But Guildenstern loved Osric;
All here above were abused by Love,
So why say, "Alas, poor Yorick!""

✳

Georgy-Porgy pudding and pie
Kissed the girls and made them cry.
You, like him, are just riff-raff;
Make me cry? You make me laugh!

Waves of desire
Ebb and flow
What's constant is
The undertow

*

A girl learns the virtue of "No, not yet,"
That it's much wiser to play hard to get.
Once the ripe fruit's plucked it soon turns rotten;
She'll have to play hard to have been gotten.

*

I'd love to play with you awhile,
Indulging your love-spell on me,
If you weren't, my dear, a juvenile,
And this thus weren't a felony.

*

I lust for your body but
You'd have me love your mind:
I'd like to ask God why he put
Your brains in your behind.

A notch or three
On many a belt,
The field's played me,
I've played the felt.

*

Aphrodite's lack of arms
Was her fundamental charm;
You have instead Athena's strength
To thus hold me at arm's-length.

*

How to treat the heat caused by desire?
Avoid both the frying-pan and the fire!
Invariably one's flame-broiled and charred,
Or one simmers slowly in tepid lard.

*

Narcissus swoons in
Deep dejection:
His valentine's rippled
His reflection.

Love Continued

Let us quit this affray
Abominable
And be like DNA:
Recombinable.

*

"We're finitely unbounded," said Einstein:
Can't think of a better valentine.

*

"Howsoever and Whereas"
My heart you are remanding;
But I will love you regardless,
Nevertheless and notwithstanding.

*

This note I place
My heart upon
If you don't love me
Pass it on

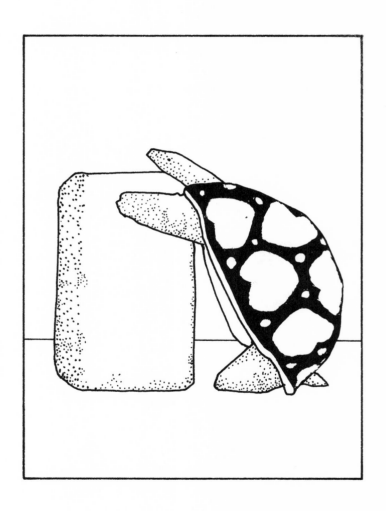

Narcissus recieved a valentine
Professing deep affection,
Saying, "I'm more thou than thine,
Yours Truly, your Reflection."

*

Love is not love which alters when it alteration finds,
Though it's often far too baggy or so tight it binds.

*

Poor Turtle's heart is not his own,
He's fallen for a paving stone;
No stronger love lives on this planet:
It lasts forever and is made of granite.

*

Roses are red,
Violets blue,
But such colors
Are not true:
My love's flowers
Must be instead
Ultra-violet,
Infra-red.

Darling, high and low you're curvy,
And I love you topsy-turvy,
Which way is up I misconstrue,
Head over heels in love with you.

*

I've surrendered.
You've reciprocated.
It's about time
We recapitulated.

*

Love is blind.
What's more endearing
Is that he's also
Hard of hearing...

*

Let's thank our stars that Love is blind
Instead of just near-sighted:
If we could see our love would be
On both sides unrequited.

It matters not how dark the night,
You shed a lingerie of light.

*

Your love's quicksand
Right to the chin
Every move I make
I'm deeper in

*

Narcissus got his
Card alright:
Gave with his left,
Took with his right.

*

Shall I compare thee to a summer's day?
You're hot and humid in a hazy sort of way.

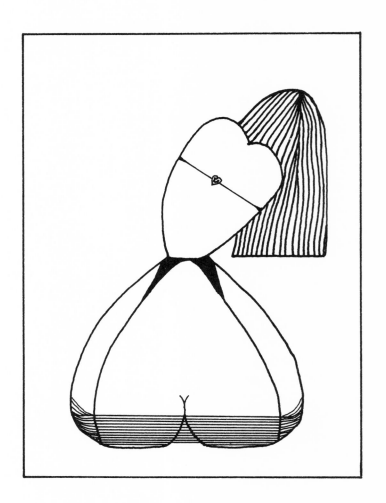

The Strap that glides across your shoulder,
The tautness that is Heaven's Holder,
The Hook that holds you in embrace,
The silk support, the Fringe of Lace,

(The sweet soft sheen of milky-white
On which the sun ne'er shone its light!)

The Hasp that lies on your pale thighs,
Clasping (the real Bridge of Sighs)
The Filigree circling your slim waist
To the Nylon Sheer that's all but chaste,

(This lacy Belt that's Roman-arched
Is water to a tongue that's parched!)

The Silk that arches so gracefully,
High over hip to plunge to the vee,
Curving under with lustful elation
To grasp at last Hell's Justification.

(the swell and flare of your behind
Is a god's inverted Valentine!)

If I could only have my way
I'd be in all your lingerie,
I'd embrace each and every part
That is your body, but my heart!

(You turn to me with a sour grin:
"Whatever I'm wearing, you're wearing thin.")

I know why beautiful is black,
Why they call it an afro-disiac.

*

With desire's requirements
I'm tormented
Till I met you, fire had not
Been invented

*

I die twenty thousand deaths a day,
Each sight of you takes my breath away.

*

I sing "I love you," which is true,
No false note's in my melody;
By playing heart-strings as you do
You've made a lyre out of me.

Love Renounced

My love for you, fair Valentine,
Is like the oldest, finest wine:
Matured at last to final best
In the deep oak cask of my chest,
Fermenting its antique sunshine
In thinking of you, Valentine!
Decanted now in rich red drips
To complement your rose red lips;
Its bouquet seeks a sweet repose
In the delicate miracle of your nose,
Which, once inhaled, finds final rest
'Neath the twin treasures of your breast;
Its sparkle remembers your lovely eyes,
Its softness anticipates your sweet thighs;
The very cork, in thinking of you,
Invites the courtship of the corkscrew.
So drink me down and take me in,
Let my love blush on your fair skin,
Let it course through each and every part
Till it finds the bottle of your heart.

You turn away, you flick your wrist,
You order, "Perrier, with a twist."

You drone on
like sawing lumber
your honeyed words
induce but slumber
I only yawn
at your imploring
I'm not sighing
I'm just snoring
no matter how
you try to shake me
I'm fast asleep and
you won't wake me.

*

You say there are other fish in the sea,
And if that's how you feel,
I hope you catch a Great White Shark
Or at least a Moray Eel.

*

Make like a banana and split, you say?
That's okay by me; in fact, parfait.

*

I know that I swore I would love you Forever.
Could we make that Tuesday, or, whatever?

Your sweet perfume
Eludes my nose
I guess the bloom
Is off the rose.

*

You say I fit you like a glove
And that our soul's are knit,
But we've dropped a stitch, my love,
And you fit me like a mitt.

*

In fidelity
Your ex-lovers agree
(We're unanimous)
You're pusillanimous

*

Once your allure held me till dawn;
These days you only lead me yawn.

Your love? Just a passing mood.
Our eternity? Just an interlude.

*

My love's strong waves
On your shore exploded;
The tide has ebbed,
The beach, eroded...

*

Once I felt reborn in your presence.
Now what I feel is... obsolesence.

*

If you don't love me
I won't linger
Wrapped around your
Little finger
If you don't love me
Let me go
I'd not wind up as
Your yo-yo.

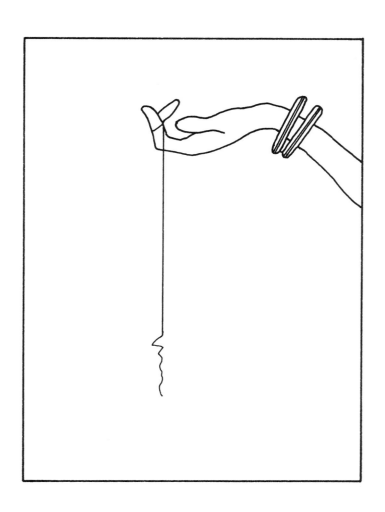

Wish I could love you,
But the sad fact is
Cupid just shoots me
For target practice.

*

You're excited by a mere illusion:
We ignited, but we'd be cold fusion.

*

You who peruse the zodiac,
Who would forsee me on my back,
Who sidles up and asks my sign
(Perhaps I'd like some more white wine?)
Pices? Virgo? Aquarius?
Concealing feelings nefarious,
You astrologer that plays the field
Should see my sign sure isn't Yield;
It'll take a lot more than Chablis
To get you into my... destiny.
Though I too am superstitious
Such foreplay is inauspicious.
Horoscope me from bottom to top,
I'll tell you what my sign is:
Stop.

Swallows returning
To Capistrano
Cycles of yearning
To you but guano

*

You're so boring
You try my patience
You've made another
Nodding acquaintance

*

I long to see more of you. For instance:
Your backside. Receding. In the distance.

*

You're a cuter, neuter, barracuda.

*

My love'll spoil:
Can't conserve it if
You insist on
No preservatives.

*I thought your love was something ethereal
When in sad fact it was merely venereal.*

*

*Cupid told me you'd be hard to do:
It's hard to hit what you see right through.*

*

*Darling, you are statuesque:
A marble heart, a stony breast.
Since you can't be moved a smidgeon
I will leave you like a pigeon.*

*

*Cupid's arrow could have been predicted:
The wound was shallow and self-inflicted.*

*

*Once I thought you a being celestial:
Now I see you're an extra-terrestial.*

Just let me say
So that you see
All that you'll lay
Is eyes on me

*

My former lust
Is lost desire,
Your nipple's just
A pacifier.
Take care lest you
Miss my meaning:
Yours the breast,
Mine, the weaning.

*

With you I thought to attain bliss
Rather than its antithesis.

*

Love is a rose but you better not picket:
You'll straddle that fence until you kick it.

"Happily" is just a word;
"Ever after" is absurd.

*

I can't say that gold
Is the color, quite,
For a whore with a heart
Of iron pyrite

*

It's close in here but the heat is trifling.
It's not that you're not hot. You're stifling.

*

My rhythm method's no nonsense:
Ain't got rhythm, got abstinence.

*

The dance floor's bare, the band's long gone:
Listen, honey: they're playing our song.

"Amor is not if it's not hot,"
The Latin lovers moan,
"Heat's not the summum bonum
But it's sure sine qua non!"

*

Your passion would not fail to please if
Your embrace weren't so self-adhesive.

*

I refuse to sing the blues
Even though I feel the urge:
Singing of my love for you
I'd have to sing a dirge.

*

Although you're shaped like an hour-glass,
That's not the seat of your femininity:
You are not so much a piece of ass
As you are a piece of assininity.

I married you
I was cuckoo
Now that I'm old
I'm a cuckold
So I'll become
A Cock-a-too
I'll change my cluck
And crow, "Cuck yoo!"

*

Once I thought you were super, thus
I'm surprised that I find you superfluous.

*

We don't entwine
We're in decline
Sweet Valentine
Won't you be thine?

*

You'd seclude me with lewd ineptitude;
My mood precludes wooed-nude interludes.

A whispered "No" is a turn-on,
Fire and powder until dawn;
Let us take a little snooze,
Then I'll re-light while you refuse.

*

Now he's laid me, gone to sleep,
But as you sow, so shall you reap:
If he should die before he wakes
I'd pray, but hey, those are the breaks.

*

If you'll have me
I'll have you
Then we'll have had each other;
And having had
We'll both be sad
And forsake one another.
So you keep yours
And I'll keep mine,
We'll send each other
Valentines.

*

Our love, in perspective, had a vanishing point.

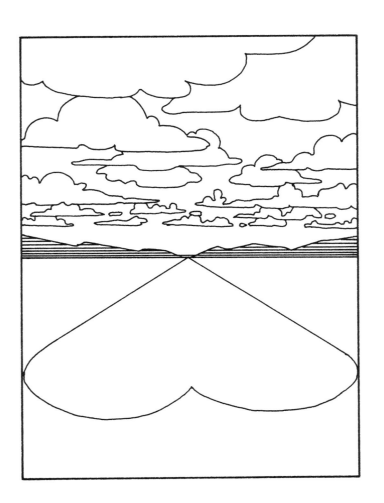

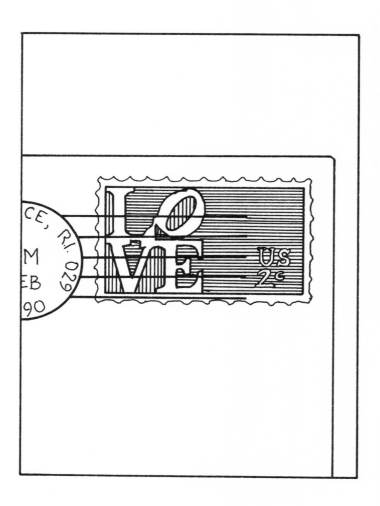

Dear John/Jane

Dear John

Your list of virtues
Is concise
You are a paragon
Of vice

You're a telephone
Without a dime
You're a back
Without a spine

As a stand-up guy
You're fetal
You're hay inside
A stack of needles

As a butterfly
You are larva
And marvelous?
More louse than marva-

At cleverness
You're not a whit
At eloquence
You're not worth spit

As a real mensch
You're merely style
As lover-boy
You're puerile

As a pencil
You're a stub
As an entrée
You are grub

As a dude
You are a dud
As fine wine
You are a Bud

As heavy breathing
You're halitosis
As a heart beating
You're thrombosis

As a necktie
You're a noose
As locomotive
You're caboose

As Mister Right
You are what's left
Kirk Douglas' chin
Without the cleft

Your caress is less
Than wonderous
Your kisses are
A blunderbuss

As a fruit
You are a kiwi
As a jock-strap
You're a pee-wee

As excitement
You are sleep
As a fast pace
You're a creep

As a love-pang
You're a prick
You're the groin
The Rockettes kick

You're a flat tire
Without a jack
To a lass
You're just alack

In terms of Time
You are a "tick"
As my "Off" switch
You are a"click"

You're a story
Without a plot
You're polio
Without the shot

Our roles are
Devoid of mystery
I am Poetry
You are History

Dear Jane

As Sugar n' Spice
You are saccharine
Everything nice you're
Wholly lacking in

You're a flower
Without petals
You're Jack's beanstalk
Made of nettles

As a pure note
You're a medley
As a femme fatale
You're deadly

As the nadir
You are tip-top
As a swan-dive
You're belly-flop

As a flame
You are a flicker
As a smile
You are a snicker

As porcelain
You're bric-a-brac
As evening-gown
You're a gunny-sack

As carpe diem
You are "Never!"
As le mot juste
You are ,"whatever... "

As a blind date
You aren't braille
You're the fee
That is in "female"

You're an itch
Without a scratch
As a red rose
You're a briar-patch

As Love Eternal
You 're a crush
As a primrose path
You're underbrush

As champagne
You are a Pepsi
As sweet dreams
You're narcolepsy

You're Plus Sizes
In birthday suits
You're as sexy as
See-through boots

As best foot forward
You are faux-pas
As an up-lift you're
A BlunderBra

As a cover - girl
You're Business Week
As savoir faire
You're up the creek

As an eye surgeon
You're scalpel slips
As circumcision
You're extra snips

As A through Z
Your letter's scarlet
You're constant as
The northern starlet

You're a magician
Without rabbits
You're a nunnery
Of nasty habits

Whoever's had you
Has been had
You're the Trojan Horse
In my Iliad

As a Siren
You are off-key
You're an asterisk
In my Odessey

Letters

Dear John:
Consider yourself flushed.

*

Dear Juan:
Hasta manyawna. Vaya con brio.

*

Dear Jean:
Liberté. Egalité: Fraternité.

*

Dear Johan:
Go fly a gemütlichkeit.

Gay Love

Saint Christopher be my guy,
A Lamp Unto My Feet,
Light my way and let's us two
Go down the St. named after you.

*

Would we have had all of this trouble
If God made not Eve but Adam's double?
Would it not have improved the text
If Noah had made the Ark single-sex?
Mankind, it's true, would be obsolete;
History would have been short, but sweet.

*

Said Jane, "This remote jungle scena
Would wipe the grin off a hyena;
Sure Tarzan can swing,
But vines are his thing;
Think I'll go bunk in with Sheena."

*

I am a lady in dis dress
I just want to be one of de guise.

Sappho, they say, lived far away
on an island remote from traffic,
courting the Muse and amusing the ewes
and avoiding all things Priapic.

Come Lady Gay, then let's away
to an island of our own,
where love is sung in an ancient tongue
and there's more than winds that moan.

*

Calling me names may disconcert me;
A stick and stones will never hurt me.

*

Charming Cupid is in a rut:
His target's always on a butt.

*

Lavender blue, dilly dilly,
Lavender you, silly silly
Lavender queen.

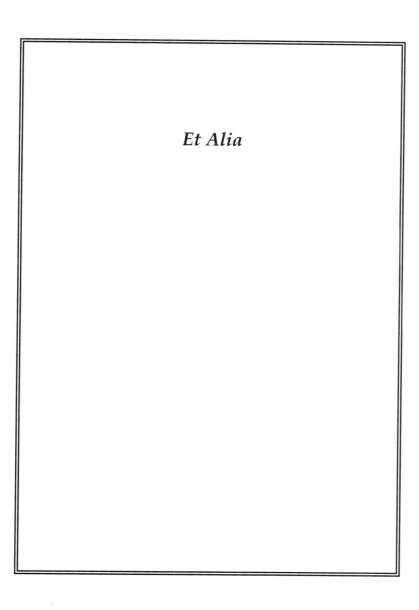

Et Alia

Too bad Darwin failed to teach us
Love is the Origin of the Specious.

*

If by Cupid
The dead were smitten
Their valentines
Would be ghost-written.

*

Against love we've
Got no defenses:
It don't make sense
But sure makes Census.

*

Omnia Vincit Amor:
Genetalia,
Et alia.

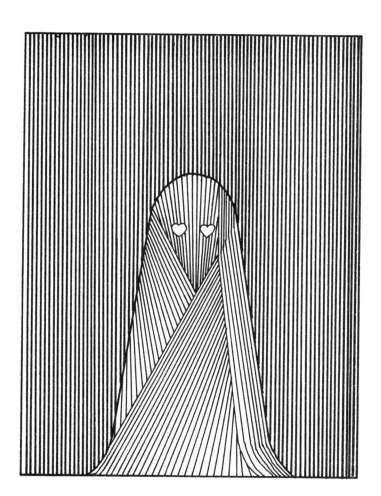